Lovely Mandalas

Copyright: Published in the United States by Orville Kyle
Published January 2017
ISBN-13: 978-1542638913
ISBN-10: 1542638917

Thank you

www.ingramcontent.com/pod-product-compliance
Lightning Source LLC
Chambersburg PA
CBHW081555280526
45788CB00011B/3476